P9-DEL-013

DATE DUE

J.

Midlothian
Public Library

14701 S. Kenton Ave.
Midlothian, IL 60445

THE
PUEBLO
INDIANS

MIDLOTHIAN PUBLIC LIBRARY
14701 S. Kenton Avenue
Midlothian, IL 60445

THE JUNIOR LIBRARY OF
AMERICAN INDIANS

THE PUEBLO INDIANS

MIDLOTHIAN PUBLIC LIBRARY
14701 S. Kenton Avenue
Midlothian, IL 60445

Liza N. Burby

CHELSEA JUNIORS
a division of CHELSEA HOUSE PUBLISHERS

FRONTISPIECE: The White House, located in the Canyon de Chelly National Monument, Arizona, is the ruin of a large dwelling built into the foot of a cliff by the Pueblos' ancestors.

CHAPTER TITLE ORNAMENT: Ancient Pueblo art, painted on rocks and cave walls, often depicted the buffalo, an important animal hunted for food and hides.

English-language words that are italicized in the text can be found in the glossary at the back of the book.

Chelsea House Publishers
EDITORIAL DIRECTOR Richard Rennert
EXECUTIVE MANAGING EDITOR Karyn Gullen Browne
COPY CHIEF Robin James
PICTURE EDITOR Adrian G. Allen
ART DIRECTOR Robert Mitchell
MANUFACTURING DIRECTOR Gerald Levine

The Junior Library of American Indians
SENIOR EDITOR Ann-Jeanette Campbell

Staff for THE PUEBLO INDIANS
TEXT EDITOR Mary B. Sisson
COPY EDITOR Catherine Iannone
EDITORIAL ASSISTANT Annie McDonnell
DESIGNER John Infantino
PICTURE RESEARCHER Sandy Jones
COVER ILLUSTRATOR Hal Just

Copyright © 1994 by Chelsea House Publishers, a division of Main Line Book Co. All rights reserved. Printed and bound in Mexico.

First Printing

1 3 5 7 9 8 6 4 2

Library of Congress Cataloging-in-Publication Data

Burby, Liza.
The Pueblo Indians / Liza Burby.
   p. cm. — (The Junior library of American Indians)
Includes index.
   ISBN 0-7910-1669-2.
        0-7910-2485-7 (pbk.)
1. Pueblo Indians—Juvenile literature. [1. Pueblo Indians. 2. Indians of North America.] I. Title. II. Series.
E99.P9B89 1994   93-40762
973'.04974—dc20   CIP
                                                         AC

CONTENTS

The ancestors of the Pueblos, the Anasazis ("Ancient Ones" in Navajo), built multi-layered villages, the remains of one seen at left, in the protected recesses of cliff walls.

CHAPTER 1

One People

In the beginning, the people lived in darkness under the earth. They came out of the underworld through a lake at the sacred place called *shipapu*. After they died they would return and reenter the underworld.

The people did not know how to survive in the new world aboveground, so the Great Spirit and the *kachinas*, or sacred beings, showed them how to build, how to hunt, and how to plant crops. One of the most important crops was corn, which grew in yellow, blue, red, white, speckled, and black. The kachinas also showed the people how to water their fields using terraces and canals and reservoirs. In return, they asked the people to honor them by performing sacred dances, which they taught to the people.

In Pueblo religious ceremonies, kachina masks like the ones shown here and on opposite page represent sacred spirits.

At this time, the people were unified, living together and speaking the same language. They built great buildings with many floors that were connected by ladders. These homes, made of stone and dried mud, were built one on top of the other and had terraces in front. Villages were built on the top of flat, tablelike hills called mesas. The people prospered.

But there was danger in the world. There were floods and tornadoes and droughts and warring enemies. With help from the kachinas, the people moved and built new, towering homes along the walls of cliffs. Here, their enemies could not reach them.

The Great Spirit, however, knew of a place that was better than the cliffs, a place with rich soil and no earthquakes, floods, droughts, or enemies. The Great Spirit showed the people the beautiful country along the Rio Grande, where the rain fell in the spring and the snow fell in the winter. The people moved to the valley of the Rio Grande, which flows from present-day Colorado to the Gulf of Mexico, and their life was agreeable. Their numbers became so great that they began to spread out into many separate villages. They even began to speak different languages from one another. But the Great Spirit and the kachinas, reminding them of all they had been through together, told them that they were one people and would be so forever.

This is the legend of how the American Indian peoples known as the Pueblos came to live in their homeland, in what is now the state of New Mexico. *Pueblo* is a Spanish

word that means village or town. It was used to describe these Indians by the first Europeans who saw their magnificent stone and *adobe* homes and villages. Since all Indians living in this area built these types of buildings, the Spanish called them all by the same name. The Pueblos are not all the same, however. Even though individual villages, or pueblos, are close to one another, each has a unique culture; the language used in each pueblo is very different from that used in neighboring pueblos.

Despite these differences, the Pueblos have a common history and ancestry that unite them as a people. Pueblo civilization is one of the oldest in North America. Pueblo ancestors, the Anasazis, or Ancient Ones, had built a civilization almost 1,000 years ago on the mesas and cliffs where the present-day states of Colorado, New Mexico, Arizona, and Utah meet. The Pueblos had already been living in their villages for hundreds of years by the time the Spanish *conquistadores* arrived in the Rio Grande valley in the middle of the 16th century. When the first Europeans entered their territory, the Pueblos were skilled farmers and shared a religion that centered around secret, circular underground rooms known as *kivas*.

Today, there are 19 remaining Pueblo villages in New Mexico. They are the Taos, Picuris, Nambe, Pojoaque, San Ildefonso, Tesuque, San Juan, Santa Clara, Jemez, Cochiti, Sandia, San Felipe, Santa Ana, Santo Domingo, Zia, Isleta, Acoma, Laguna, and Zuni pueblos. All 19 are in the northern part of the state. Except for the Zuni pueblo, which is much farther west, all the Pueblo villages in New Mexico are on the Rio Grande and its tributaries. In addition to the New Mexican Pueblos, there are a Pueblo people living in Arizona—the Hopis.

Although the New Mexican Pueblos were one of the first Native American peoples to meet non-Indians, they have been very successful at keeping their customs and identities as Indians. One important reason for this is that, unlike many other Indian tribes, the Pueblos have never been permanently forced off their land. Even today, many Pueblos still live in their original homeland, the land the Great Spirit showed them hundreds of years before white soldiers on horseback arrived from a different world across the sea. ▲

Francisco Vásquez de Coronado set out for Quivira in 1541, believing it to be a city of silver and gold. Once there, he found only grass huts.

CHAPTER 2

Cities of Silver and Gold

The Spanish first explored the lands of the Pueblo Indians, which is now called the American Southwest, in the early 16th century. They were *lured* by stories of fabulously wealthy cities told by people who had traveled farther than the Spanish explorers had. Although these storytellers usually had no evidence to prove they were telling the truth, their stories were often accepted as fact.

One such report was made in 1536. During a Spanish sailing expedition from Mexico to Florida, a shipwreck occurred off the coast of what is known today as Texas. The four men who survived the wreck spent the next eight years wandering among the many Indian groups who lived in the area. They finally found their way back to Mexico City, and their leader, Álvar Núñez Cabeza de Vaca, claimed that during their wanderings the four men had seen "large and powerful villages, four and five stories high." These stories interested the *viceroy* of Mexico, Don Antonio de Mendoza, who decided to organize an expedition to the north to find these villages, which he thought would be in a region the Indians called Cíbola.

A Franciscan priest named Fray Marcos de Niza led the expedition, which included one of the four survivors of the shipwreck, a Moor named Esteban. Fray Marcos was instructed by the viceroy to learn all he could about Cíbola, to claim the land in the name of the king of Spain, and to convert all the natives to Christianity. The expedition left for Cíbola on March 7, 1539.

Esteban led a small party that went ahead of the larger group. They reached the Zuni pueblo of Hawikuh in west-central New Mexico. When the party arrived, Esteban explained to the Zunis that the Spanish had come "to establish peace and to heal them." He did not seem to notice that neither he nor his party was welcome. Instead, Esteban bragged about the size and the military skills of the expedition that was following not far behind him. According to a Yuma Indian who told the tale two years later to another group of Spanish invaders, the Zunis "killed him and tore him into many pieces . . . so that he would not reveal their location to his brothers."

When Fray Marcos heard the news, he quickly returned to Mexico. Though many people correctly doubted the friar had seen Hawikuh at all, he gave a glowing description of the pueblo, saying it was bigger than Mexico City. Spanish excitement about Cíbola grew. Viceroy Mendoza publicly announced that Cíbola had been discovered and made plans to conquer it. He put Francisco Vásquez de Coronado in command of a new Spanish force to make the perilous journey from Mexico to Hawikuh. While traveling, they heard a message that the Zunis had sent out among the tribes: If the Spanish pass your way, you "should not respect them, but kill them."

The Zunis at Hawikuh were waiting for Coronado and his men when they came to the pueblo in early June 1540. The women and children hid at the top of a nearby mesa. Only the warriors and several older men, who served as war captains, remained to defend the village. The Spaniards stood outside the pueblo walls while one of them read aloud a demand that the Indians obey the Christian god and the king of Spain. The Zunis' answer was a shower of arrows. But the Spanish were in armor and on horseback, and they had guns, which the Indians called "canes that spit fire and made thunder." The Spanish captured Hawikuh, but much to their disappointment, did not find the gold and silver they had expected. Despite this setback, they were impressed both by evidence of the Indians' skills as farmers and by the Indians' elaborate stone and adobe buildings, some of which were seven stories high.

Word quickly spread among the Pueblos that Hawikuh had been conquered by fierce men who rode terrible beasts that were rumored to eat people (like all Indians, the Pueblos had never seen horses before the Europeans came). Each pueblo reacted differently to the Spanish. Most of the Indians offered the newcomers signs of peace, but the Hopis and Acomas warned the Spaniards not to cross symbolic boundary lines they had drawn in the earth. Coronado's soldiers were better-armed than the Indians and swept aside all resistance. The Spanish advanced east to a province called Tiguex, where the majority of the pueblos were located.

MIDLOTHIAN PUBLIC LIBRARY

Zuni Indians tried to protect the pueblo of Hawikuh from Spanish invaders, but their courage and arrows proved no match for the Spaniards' guns and horses.

One soldier, Pedro de Castaneda, described the Pueblo life in Tiguex. He reported how the Pueblos made cementlike mortar of charcoal, ash, and dirt, and he was impressed by the underground kivas, saying some were so large "they could be used for a game of ball." Castaneda also admired the

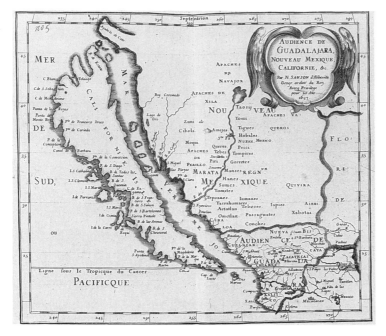

This French map of the American Southwest, drawn in 1657, gives the names of several pueblos in "Nouveau Mexique."

Pueblos' cleanliness, their beautiful clay jars (which are still made today), and their willingness to work together. But the natives of Tiguex were not willing to work with their would-be conquerers, and they rebelled. The Spanish stopped the uprising with extreme brutality, burning Indians at the stake, and overtaking two pueblos. The Indians retreated to the mesa tops and abandoned their villages to the conquistadores.

Because the Spanish army was too strong for the Indians to defeat in battle, the Pueblos tried to get rid of the invaders through cleverness. An Indian prisoner told his captors tales of silver and gold in a city to the east called

Quivira. Coronado and his men believed him and made a long journey across the plains, looking for Quivira. When they found it, they discovered that it was nothing more than a group of grass huts in what is today the state of Kansas. Under torture, their prisoner revealed that the people of the Cicuye pueblo had asked him to lead the Spaniards on a wild-goose chase. Their hope was that the Spaniards would get lost, run out of food, and become too weak to fight.

Coronado returned disappointed from Quivira to Pueblo country and stayed there for another winter. In the two years the Spaniards had explored the area, they had found none of the riches they had hoped for. They returned to Mexico in the spring of 1542 empty-handed, leaving two Franciscan friars behind to preach Christianity to the Indians. The friars were killed as soon as the army left. When the viceroy heard Coronado's report, he was so unhappy he declared that no one should ever speak of the expedition again. For the time being, the mysterious north had lost its attraction for the Spanish. The Indians were left alone to live their centuries-old way of life. ▲

*Two Tewa Indian
girls model traditional
clothing. Their hair is
wrapped around
wooden molds in
the shape of squash
blossoms—a sign that
they are unmarried.*

CHAPTER 3

Fear, Friendship, and Hatred

Thirty-nine years after Coronado returned to Mexico, a new Spanish expedition, organized to convert the Pueblos to Christianity, started out for the Rio Grande valley. The explorers soon discovered that the Indians had not forgotten the Spanish. The Pueblos retreated to the mountains and hid until the expedition sent word that it had come in peace.

During the several months that the expedition was in Pueblo country, it explored 57 pueblos. A man named Gallegos kept notes, saying that at first the Indians were very generous and gave the Spanish so much food that each day there was enough left over to feed 500 men. But the Spanish soon wore out their welcome, demanding more and more food from the Indians as their own supplies *dwindled*. Soon they were forcing all the pueblos to give them food, supplies, and shelter.

The Spanish fooled themselves into believing that the Pueblos were pleased to give them the tribute of food and supplies that they demanded. Soon it became clear how the Indians really felt. In September, a solitary Spanish friar left for Mexico to report on the expedition's progress. The Pueblos followed the friar and killed him. Frightened, the remaining members of the expedition decided to return to Mexico, but three friars stayed behind to preach the gospel to the natives.

When the soldiers were repeatedly attacked during their return to Mexico, they realized that the friars left behind were probably in grave danger. Upon the soldiers' arrival in Mexico, a party led by Don Antonio de Espejo set off to rescue the clergymen, but the friars had been killed soon after the soldiers had left.

Espejo observed the Pueblos carefully on his mission and noted in his journal that more

In 1581, a Spanish chronicler wrote a description of the Pueblos' snake dance. Centuries later, when this photograph was taken, the dance was still being performed.

than 12,000 Indians lived in apartmentlike homes on either side of the Rio Grande. The men wore cotton blankets, buffalo hides, or chamois skins, while the women wore cotton skirts, often embroidered with colored threads, and a blanket over their shoulders fastened at the waist by a strip of embroidered material with tassels. Both men and women wore deerskin shoes with soles of buffalo hide.

Espejo recorded Pueblo religious practices, but he and his men were hostile to the Indian religion because it was different from the Catholicism they knew. The Spanish called the Pueblo gods and kachinas "devils." Espejo wrote in his journal:

> In every one of these pueblos there is a house to which food is brought for the devil. The natives have small stone idols which they worship; and also, just as the Spanish have crosses along the roads, these people set up . . . wayside shrines where they place painted sticks and feathers, saying that the devil will stop there to rest and talk to them.

Espejo assured the Pueblos that he and his men had come in peace. He was so convincing that the Pueblos overwhelmed the visitors with a feast of rabbit, venison, tortillas, *atole* (a soft drink made of maize flour), beans, calabashes, and corn. But as the other Spanish conquistadores had done, Espejo and his men soon began to place

Kivas—large, usually circular, underground chambers—were built for religious ceremonies and to represent the Pueblos' mythological home.

demands on the Pueblos. They went from pueblo to pueblo, asking repeatedly for food, turquoise, gold, and silver. When they did not receive what they wanted, they began to torture and kill the Indians and burn their pueblos.

In retaliation for these actions, Pueblo warriors began to frequently attack Espejo's party. After several skirmishes, Espejo realized that his relatively small band of men could not hold off the Indians indefinitely. He returned to Mexico in 1583 and reported to the viceroy that the Rio Grande valley was a rich place for a Spanish colony.

In December of 1590, Gaspar Costano de Sosa led an expedition of settlers to the pueblo of Cicuye, along the Pecos River. After their recent experience with Espejo, the Pueblos assumed that these Spanish were also hostile. They attacked a Spanish advance party, taking their supplies. When de Sosa marched on Cicuye with a larger group to get the goods back, he found the Indians waiting to do battle. De Sosa initially tried *diplomacy,* but the Indians had no goodwill left for the Spanish, and a battle began. Spanish firepower won out and the invaders took control of the pueblo.

To their amazement, the Spanish soon discovered that the beautifully designed city they had won was deserted. The Indians had disappeared into a maze of underground tunnels they had built and slipped out of the pueblo. When the Spanish entered the maze, they discovered 16 very large whitewashed kivas, or circular underground rooms. Aboveground, the town had five plazas, two community water holes for bathing, and separate springs for drinking water. Each house was well stocked, having two or more rooms full of corn, as well as herbs, chiles, and gourds. There was plenty of firewood and lumber, farming equipment, and pottery such as bowls and cups.

Any further exploration on de Sosa's part came to a sudden end when he was arrested by Spanish soldiers. He had never received permission from the viceroy to establish a colony, so he and his expedition had to return to Mexico.

The Pueblos had only a short break from the Spanish settlers, however. Another group of settlers, led by Don Juan de Oñate, followed the Rio Grande north and arrived in 1598 to colonize the area. When Oñate sent armed men ahead to take supplies from the Indians, the Pueblos realized they could not win against Spanish guns and fled to the mountains. The Spanish took what they wanted from the abandoned homes, finally settling in the deserted pueblo of San Gabriel, across the river from what is today San Juan, New Mexico. There, the Spanish colonists suffered from the harsh weather that characterizes the Rio Grande area: "eight months of winter and four months of hell."

Despite the weather, the Spanish were determined to make the land yield riches—preferably without using Spanish labor. They decided to intimidate the Pueblos into working for them. Oñate held a meeting with the tribal elders in the pueblo of Santo Domingo, where he told them "it was greatly to their advantage that, of their own free will . . . they render obedience and submission [to the Spanish]." The Pueblo leaders understood that, if they resisted, they would at best be forced to live as fugitives in the mountains, while if they accepted Oñate's terms, they would be able to return to their pueblos and their farms. The elders agreed that the Pueblos would work for the Spanish without pay, tending their fields and gardens, caring for their livestock, and repairing their homes. Pueblos who refused were tortured.

Because the crops grown by the Pueblos for the Spanish were insufficient to feed the San Gabriel colony, each month the Spanish soldiers demanded more of the Pueblos' food. They even took what had been stockpiled for times of hardship. Inevitably, drought came and dried up the cornfields. With no remaining reserves, famine soon followed, sparking a number of Pueblo uprisings which were viciously suppressed by the Spanish.

Even with the Pueblos' labor, the Spanish found life in their colony harder than they had expected. When Oñate left the colony in 1601 to take a trip east, three-quarters of the disappointed Spanish colonists returned to Mexico. The viceroy in Mexico City, hearing reports of brutality and starvation in the colcolony, recalled Oñate in 1610. For a short while, the Indians were left alone. ◣

This 1935 photograph of a Pueblo deer dancer proves the ultimate failure of the Spanish to destroy Pueblo culture and convert the Indians to Roman Catholicism.

CHAPTER 4

The Great Missionary Era

After Oñate was recalled, the Spanish declared Pueblo country a royal colony, which meant that settlers were under the protection of the Spanish king. The stated purpose of the settlement was, again, to convert the Pueblos to Christianity. This period, which marks the height of Spanish power in New Mexico, became known to the Spanish as the Great Missionary Era—but to the Indians, it was a time of great hardship.

The Spanish were still interested in profiting from their colony, but instead of the unorganized tributes that were collected under Oñate, the Spanish colonial government

Under the encomendero system, Pueblos were forced to work virtually as slaves for the Spanish soldiers, keeping house, herding animals, and tending gardens such as this one.

created the *encomendero* system. *Encomiendas*, or land grants, were given to Spanish soldiers as payment for five years of service and were usually located close to a pueblo. Under a peculiar Spanish law, the soldiers were not actually supposed to live on the land they had been granted but could make money from it by receiving tribute—such as cotton blankets and corn—from the Indians who lived around the grant areas. The soldiers had the right to force the Pueblos who lived near their encomiendas to work for them as herders, field hands, and servants. Interestingly enough, the Spanish law that allowed the soldiers essentially to enslave the Pueblos also stated that the soldiers had to pay them in Spanish currency. Even this small amount of legal protection for the Pueblos was routinely ignored, however, and Indian laborers were usually unpaid, unfed, and brutally treated.

By 1621, tales of widespread mistreatment of the Pueblos in New Mexico reached colonial authorities in Mexico City, who issued decrees regulating the kind of work the Spanish could force the Indians to do. But authorities in Mexico City were a long way from New Mexico, and the Spanish soldiers (along with many New Mexican government officials) simply ignored the new laws, withholding wages, abusing workers, and causing severe labor shortages in the pueblos.

The Spanish clergy also benefited from *extorted* Indian labor. Missions were built by Pueblo Indians, at great human cost, in six Pueblo villages. Dishonest clergymen used unpaid Indians as shepherds and farmers, pocketing profits from livestock and crops that, under church policy, were to be used to feed the native people in times of famine. The clergy forced Pueblos to work in their homes as horsemen, cooks, gardeners, and maids, and in their churches as translators, bell ringers, and choir members.

The friars were infamous for being more interested in teaching the Pueblos how to be good servants than how to be good Catholics. As a result, most Indians received only limited religious instruction, learning to honor the symbol of the cross, to respect the clergy, to say simple prayers, and to receive the basic sacraments. Despite this casual attitude toward religious education, the friars were *adamant* that the Pueblos attend mass, and they brutally persecuted Pueblos who practiced their native religion, calling it sorcery. Indians had their heads shaved, were whipped, or were kept in stocks when they did not go to church, and many were cruelly executed for practicing their own religion.

Not surprisingly, the Indians continued to practice their traditional ceremonies and resented the missionaries' attempts to force a new religion upon them. They expressed their displeasure and contempt in a number of ways. Sometimes, the Pueblos resisted the missionaries with humor—Indian translators might mimic the priests or change their words to funny curses. Other times, the resistance turned violent. Friars who overly antagonized the Pueblos sometimes found themselves the victims of local uprisings. By 1640, some pueblos were so dangerous that a priest's assignment there was considered a grave and life-threatening punishment.

continued on page 41

THE OLDEST ARCHITECTS

Rumors of Pueblo villages filled with treasure tempted the Spanish conquistadores to conquer Pueblo lands and peoples. While the Spanish did not find the riches they expected, they discovered the complexity and grace of the Pueblo adobe. Instead of cities built of gold, they found cities that reflected the creativity, skill, and practicality of a civilization that developed long before the Europeans arrived in America.

The Pueblos' architecture was almost certainly a cultural inheritance from their ancestors, the Anasazis, or Ancient Ones. The Anasazis built huge adobe, tufa (a porous rock), and sandstone buildings with numerous rooms and multiple stories in the walls of cliffs or atop mesas. Although later Pueblo dwellings were made of the same materials, they tended to be smaller. The low, flat-roofed style of the Pueblo dwellings along the Rio Grande still strongly influences southwestern architecture today. Above all, the traditional buildings of the Pueblos demonstrate the lasting beauty of their culture.

Metates—stones used for grinding corn—inside an Indian ruin. Corn was the Pueblos' most important staple; most Pueblo dwellings would include rooms for its storage.

Ancient Indian petroglyphs. The Pueblos had a highly developed and extremely complex civilization long before Europeans came to the New World.

Anasazi ruins at the Hovenweep National Monument in Utah.

The famous White House Ruin in Canyon de Chelly, Arizona. No one knows for certain why the Anasazi migrated from their canyons in the Four Corners area. Raids by hostile tribes and shortages of water and wood are the most likely explanation.

Anasazi ruins in Mesa Verde National Park. During the golden age of the Anasazi, which lasted from the 11th to the 14th century, they abandoned their mesa-top villages in favor of impregnable cliffside dwellings.

The north pueblo at Taos, which is about 600 years old.

Modern doors and windows on a home in the north pueblo at Taos.

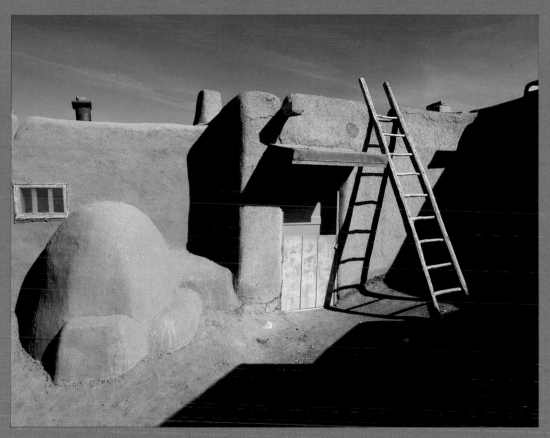

The structure to the left of the front door of this home in Taos pueblo is a bread oven made of adobe.

The entranceway to the courtyard of the old church at Taos pueblo. The Pueblo cultural heritage today includes many traditions of Hispanic origin, among them a nominal belief in Roman Catholicism. In recent years, some inhabitants of Taos have become practitioners of the peyote religion.

continued from page 32

The Great Missionary Era brought devastating changes to the Pueblos. Epidemics of European diseases, especially smallpox, swept through the villages every 10 to 12 years. A number of droughts brought famine to the Pueblos, and in the mid-1600s, damaging raids by Apache and Navajo Indians began. Because of their advanced farming and irrigation techniques, the Pueblos could often grow crops in hard times, but these crops made tempting targets for raids. Sometimes, however, the raiders wanted revenge against the Spanish who took peaceful Apache and Navajo traders as slaves. Since the Pueblos supported the Spanish settlers (albeit unwillingly), their communities were made to pay for this Spanish treachery and were attacked again and again, until entire pueblos had to be abandoned.

Famine, disease, Spanish cruelty, and Apache and Navajo raids caused the Pueblo population to decrease. At the beginning of the 17th century, there were about 50,000 Pueblo Indians. Seven decades later, there were only about 17,000. The Pueblos decided that they had brought this hardship upon themselves by accepting certain elements of Spanish religion and culture. So, in the early 1670s, the Indians returned to their

own traditions. As a result, the Spanish became more determined to do away with native practices. The friars stepped up their attempt to eradicate Pueblo religion, seizing control of the kivas, destroying ritual masks, costumes, and prayer sticks, and killing and torturing Pueblo "sorcerers."

This persecution backfired, however. The Pueblos, led by Popé, a Tewa Indian from the pueblo of San Juan, planned a unified uprising to drive the Spanish from New Mexico. On August 10, 1680, the Pueblo quickly overran the Spanish settlements in the Rio Grande valley, and by August 21, 1680, the Spanish had abandoned the city of Santa Fe. The Pueblos wanted to drive the Spanish from

The Pueblos had to pay tribute to their conquerers, often in the form of goods such as woven blankets. In addition, the Pueblos were expected to honor the symbols of Roman Catholicism.

their lands, but not to massacre them, so casualties were light—except among the missionaries. The Pueblos were so angered by the missionaries that they set fire to all missionary buildings, including churches, along with records of religious ceremonies such as baptisms.

Famine and drought did not leave with the Spanish, however, and without the protection of the Spanish troops, the Apache attacks worsened. Caught between these forces, many pueblos had to be abandoned. After Popé died in 1688, the Pueblo peoples found it hard to remain unified. In 1692, a number of Indians asked the Spanish to return. Spanish general Diego de Vargas reclaimed Santa Fe with a small force. This time, what little fighting there was occurred between Pueblos: those who opposed the Spanish and those who supported them. By 1696, all the remaining inhabited pueblos, except for those of the Hopis, were once again under Spanish rule. ▲

*At the beginning of the
17th century, Pueblos
and Spaniards accepted
their need of each other;
their cooperation was
peaceful and bountiful,
but also imperfect.*

CHAPTER 5

A Time of Cooperation

On a cold day in January 1706, a new Spanish governor summoned Pueblo leaders to Santa Fe for a historic meeting. The Indians had come to realize that they needed the military protection provided by Spanish troops, while the 1680 rebellion made the colonists understand that their physical survival in New Mexico depended upon the Pueblos' goodwill. Both the Pueblos and the Spanish acknowledged that they would have to cooperate and work together in order to live.

The encomendero system was ended. Tributes and forced labor were replaced

by trade between the Spanish and the Indians. Spanish abuses of the Indians did not
end with the age of cooperation, but authorities, eager to avoid antagonizing Pueblo
communities, were more likely to listen to the
Pueblos' complaints. Pueblos who had been
forced to work as herdsmen, cowboys, and
blacksmiths under the Spanish now used
these skills to further enrich their own communities. Labor needed to keep up irrigation
ditches was sometimes shared with Spanish
settlers. Pueblo farmers raised crops and
livestock brought by the Spanish, along with
native crops. Pueblo farming was much
more productive now than during the Great
Missionary Era—in no small part because the
Pueblos were assured that they could keep
the fruits of their labor.

The Spanish church in Pueblo country had
been weakened by the revolt of 1680. By
1776, there were only 20 priests in all of New
Mexico; Spanish missionaries are believed to
have converted no more than 5,000 Pueblos
to Christianity in the entire 18th century. The
Pueblos had learned to speak Spanish so
they could trade with the newcomers, but
they kept their native languages. In the same
way, some Pueblos accepted certain parts of
Christianity but kept their native faith (wisely
keeping it hidden from the Spanish). The

While many Pueblos gave the appearances of being Christian, their native religious practices survived into the 20th century, as shown in this 1930 deer dance.

Hopis resisted Christianity more than the other Pueblos, and their settlements became home to many Pueblo rebels who wanted little to do with the Spanish.

While religion caused some problems between the Spanish and the Pueblos, military needs brought them together. By the 1730s, there was a new, fearsome enemy—the Comanches. They joined the Navajos, Utes, and Apaches in raiding the Spanish and Pueblo settlements. The Spanish garrison at Santa Fe had less than 100 men, and Spanish authorities relied on Pueblo *auxiliaries* to hold the raiding tribes at bay. As a result, Spanish restrictions on Indian ownership of firearms and horses were dropped.

At first, the Pueblo military was kept separate from the Spanish military, but by the latter half of the century this practice was abandoned. "Spanish" expeditions were often 75 to 85 percent Pueblo, with Pueblos serving not only as warriors, but also as spies, scouts, interpreters, and messengers.

The officers in these expeditions were always Spanish, but Pueblo war captains commanded their own men. In addition, Pueblo villages served as meeting places and supplied fighting troops with food and equipment. In return for their service and help, the Pueblos expected to recapture loved ones and valuable livestock taken by raiders, to share in war booty, and to feel secure at home in their pueblos.

In spite of cooperation between the Spanish and the Pueblos, by the 1770s the attacks by other Indian tribes had become unbearable. Some Spanish settlers left the countryside to seek safety in Santa Fe, while others took refuge among their Pueblo neighbors at Taos. In many areas, farmland had to be abandoned because it was unsafe for men to tend to their crops. As a result, hunger again visited Pueblo country. In the last quarter of the 18th century, the Pueblos were devastated once more by famine and smallpox epidemics. Village after village suffered a severe decrease in population or was completely abandoned until only 19 of the 66 Rio Grande pueblos first described by the Spaniards remained.

Finally, after a series of military victories in which the Pueblos took part, the Spanish made a truce with the hostile tribes, and the

The Pueblos' distinctive terraced villages are a fitting symbol of the Indians' steadfastness, even after centuries of conflict with their Spanish conquerors.

Pueblo population began to recover. In the eyes of the Spanish, the Pueblos had gained prestige by their defense of the province and had earned a secure place in New Mexican society. Despite the pitfalls of their alliance with the Spanish, during the 18th century the Pueblos successfully resisted exploitation, defended their homeland, and maintained their independence as a people. ▲

The 19th century saw the Pueblos under Spanish, then Mexican, and finally, U.S. rule. While the Indians adapted to more non-Indian ways, they influenced Western culture in return.

CHAPTER 6

Under Mexican Rule

In the first decades of the 19th century, the Spanish government was too busy with political events in Europe to pay much attention to the Pueblos or New Mexico. By 1812, only 121 Spanish soldiers were assigned to New Mexico to defend a population of 40,000. Though the Comanches were now at peace, other hostile Indian tribes raided the settlements continuously. The territory had a new threat as well. The Louisiana Purchase had just increased the United States's borders beyond the Mississippi River to New Mexico, and the new republic wanted to expand even further. In this uncertain political situation, the

Spanish and the Pueblos of New Mexico were forced into an even closer alliance.

Trade with the Comanches was important to the New Mexican economy. Pueblo traders ventured east to the plains, where the Comanches lived, taking with them bread, cornmeal, flour, sugar candy, onions, tobacco, iron arrows, and lance points. They traded these with Comanches for horses, mules, buffalo robes, and meat. Although

During Spanish rule, the Pueblos held their ceremonies—such as the buffalo dance pictured here—in secret, but under Mexican authority they were allowed to celebrate their rituals openly.

other Pueblos looked down on these traders for dealing with a known enemy, their trade was essential to the Pueblo economy and helped to keep the peace.

On February 9, 1811, the Spanish government proclaimed legal equality between the Spaniards and the Pueblos. Although this decree gave the Pueblos full rights as Spanish citizens under Spanish law, it took away the special legal protection of their land. Until then, a certain amount of land surrounding each pueblo had been set aside for the Indians and could not be touched by the Spanish government. Now officials complained that this area was too large for the declining Pueblo population and claimed that the land should be opened for Spanish settlement. The Spanish began to help themselves to this land, and in 1812 and 1813, new laws allowed up to half of the Indian lands to be taken by the Spanish.

Then, in 1821, New Mexico fell under the authority of the independent nation of Mexico, which had obtained its freedom from Spain. Mexican law did not help the Indians regarding land ownership, but the Mexican government indirectly helped to strengthen the Pueblo religion by not supporting the Spanish missionaries. This left the Pueblos free to pursue their rich ceremonial life and customs that had secretly helped them through the many bad years.

To the newly formed Mexican government, New Mexico was remote, unprofitable, and not much of a concern. Government officials were indifferent to the activities of the Pueblos, and allowed them to pursue their own interests without government interference. The result was a resurgence of Pueblo culture. Despite centuries of Spanish contact, the Pueblos had preserved their traditional

Pottery and woven baskets identifiable by their sharp geometric patterns remain trademarks of the Pueblos.

architecture, arts, dress, foods, and customs to such an extent that early 19th-century descriptions of Pueblo life are markedly similar to those made by the first Spanish conquistadores.

The Mexican government never adopted the policy of disarming the Pueblos or restricting their movements. As a result, traditional Pueblo hunting thrived. Every June and October, the Pueblos held buffalo hunts where they would kill 5,000 to 6,000 of the shaggy beasts. Buffalo meat was an important part of the Pueblos' diet, and the heavy coats of the buffalo killed in winter were used to make clothing or were traded with other tribes. The Pueblos hunted eagles, capturing them and keeping them alive to use their feathers to decorate clothing and to make arrows. Many Indians believed that arrows made with eagle feathers had a special ability to cut the air. The Pueblos traded these valuable arrows with other tribes for horses.

The rural Mexicans in New Mexico and the Pueblos were both neglected by the Mexican government, so they came to rely on each other for such necessary tasks as keeping irrigation ditches in good order. Because of this, the bond between the two communities grew.

Mexican families were welcome guests at Pueblo feast days, and Pueblo dancers performed in Santa Fe in full costume at annual Mexican independence day celebrations. The Mexican population took on many elements of Pueblo life. Since there were few doctors, the settlers relied on native medicines. Tortillas, atole, pinole, chile, and frijoles were food staples for both groups. Mexicans often used Pueblo pottery to cook with, and they highly valued Pueblo wicker jugs and baskets, which were so tightly woven that they were waterproof.

The Pueblos and the Mexicans also came together to protect the region from Navajo, Apache, and Ute attacks, which increased until the New Mexico settlements began to feel as threatened as before the Comanche peace treaty of the late 1700s.

Not all Pueblos became close to the Mexican community, however. The Hopi and Zuni pueblos did not interact frequently with the Mexicans, in part because these pueblos were geographically isolated and in part because frequent Apache and Navajo raids made them dangerous to visit. With the exception of fur trappers and the occasional American military expedition, few non-Indian outsiders visited the Zuni or Hopi lands.

Despite epidemics of typhoid and smallpox that killed 10 percent of the Pueblo population between 1837 and 1840, the first half of the 19th century was the least tragic period of time for the Pueblos since the Spanish first arrived. The Pueblos not only lived at peace with their Mexican neighbors but they also strongly influenced Mexican life in the region. As the Americans were to discover, a distinctly New Mexican culture, profoundly affected by Pueblo traditions, had been created. ▲

Fifty years after New Mexico was proclaimed a U.S. territory, this Hopi man was employed as a mail rider, a job glorified by the Pony Express.

CHAPTER 7

A Heavy American Hand

On August 13, 1846, American troops marched unchallenged into Santa Fe and claimed New Mexico for the United States. The Mexican War between the United States and Mexico was already under way, and the Mexicans thought that fighting over the outlying territory of New Mexico would be a waste of troops. In 1848, Mexico ceded New Mexico to the United States, and in 1850, New Mexico was officially declared a U.S. territory.

With the Americans came new questions about the exact legal status of the Pueblos in relation to their land. The United States was in a period of aggressive territorial expansion and had obtained New Mexico so that American settlers could inhabit the area. The Americans did not recognize Indian land rights and customarily forced Indians onto reservations far from their homes in order to free desirable Indian land for non-Indian settlers. It seemed likely that the Pueblos would lose their centuries-old homeland, as did many other tribes under American rule.

Pueblo leaders quickly pledged their loyalty to the United States. They had little choice: the large number of well-armed Americans made it impossible for the Pueblos to drive them off the land, and the Americans seemed unwilling to work together with the Pueblos, as the Spanish had in the early 1700s. Fortunately, the first U.S. Indian agent in New Mexico, James Calhoun, thought that moving the Pueblos to a reservation would be disastrous for New Mexico. He saw their well-built houses and their productive farms and realized that the Pueblos were too important to the local economy to be forced to leave.

The U.S. government, however, did not legally recognize the Pueblos' ownership of the land they had long used for agriculture, grazing, and settlement. Because the Pueblos were settled farmers rather than nomadic

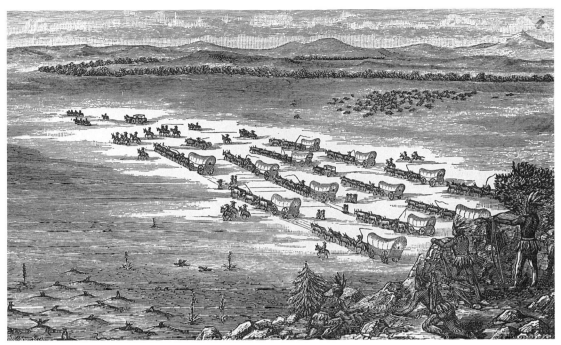

The settlers ventured into Pueblo territory in caravans of prairie schooners, otherwise known as covered wagons. Their arrival sparked decades of dispute over land rights.

hunters like many other Indians, the U.S. government decided that the Pueblos' land did not require the legal protection that reservations were given. Although the U.S. government did grant the Pueblos some land, it was not enough to support the growing Indian population. Non-Indian settlers swiftly moved into Pueblo territory.

The Americans' sheep and cattle destroyed Pueblo farmland by overgrazing. Logging companies stripped the mountains of timber, causing heavy runoff from the rains and melting snow in the spring. This, in turn, caused devastating flooding of the Pueblo lands along the Rio Grande.

The American frontier also brought with it some of the less desirable members of society. A popular scam of the rough fortune seekers on their way to California was to pretend to be government officials. They took livestock and other supplies from the Indians and promised that the government would pay them back. These swindles hit the Zuni Indians the hardest because their pueblos were located near important trade routes.

The Pueblos had other quarrels with the Americans. The U.S. Army said it would protect the Pueblos against attacks from other tribes, but it did not *deploy* enough troops to do a good job, and it forbade the Pueblos to obtain guns or to fight for themselves. Unlike the Spanish, the Americans rarely called on Pueblo troops, and when they did, they did not pay these troops well. The Hopis, isolated from the eastern settlements, suffered the most from these policies. The neighboring Navajos attacked regularly, and by 1846, the Hopi population had dwindled to about 2,450. In 1850 and again in 1851, the Hopi villages sent delegations to Santa Fe to obtain aid from the U.S. government. Help never came. In the 1860s, drought and a smallpox epidemic made their situation even more serious, and many Hopi families sought shelter with the Zunis.

After refusing to help the Pueblos defend their homes against the Navajos, the U.S. government grew concerned that the Pueblos would join forces with the Comanches, Kiowas, Cheyennes, and Arapahos. The Pueblos had frequently hunted buffalo and traded with these Plains tribes. Government officials talked about putting a stop to all contact between these tribes; finally the possibility of such an Indian alliance ended when the Plains tribes were forcibly confined to reservations and American hunters almost eliminated the buffalo population.

The slaughter of buffalo by the Americans resulted in the Pueblos being cut off from an important source of meat. But, while traditional hunting became more difficult, agriculture was getting easier. The U.S. government felt that agriculture, as opposed to hunting, was a "civilized" pursuit for the Indians and actively encouraged farming. Special government officials were assigned to Pueblo communities to introduce new farm technologies. While Pueblo crops and techniques did not change much, the Indians quickly learned to use American equipment, such as plows, shovels, hoes, rakes, pitchforks, and spring wagons. By the 1870s, the Pueblos were able to get government funds to help them build dams and wells and improve their irrigation ditches.

New tools were just some of the many and varied American items that had been arriving in Pueblo country since the opening of the Santa Fe Trail in 1822. A caravan of goods, numbering up to 100 wagons, usually arrived in July, bringing such articles as cheaply made cotton and woolen cloth, and metal and china vessels. Unfortunately, the availability of these American goods meant that Pueblo crafts such as pottery and weaving no longer sold well.

Pueblo homes and villages began to change physically under American rule. Originally, the Pueblos had covered windows in their homes with small panes of *mica*, but American window glass began to appear in Pueblo homes in the late 1870s. Windows and doors were added to ground-floor rooms, while ladders and upper-story homes began to disappear. As raids by other Indians began to slacken in the 1870s, Pueblo families moved closer to the fields they worked, creating small satellite villages away from the main pueblo compound.

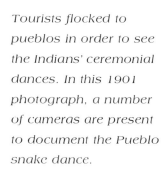

Tourists flocked to pueblos in order to see the Indians' ceremonial dances. In this 1901 photograph, a number of cameras are present to document the Pueblo snake dance.

By the end of the 19th century, the Pueblos had adapted to much of the newcomers' way of life without losing their own. The Pueblos were luckier than most Indians because the U.S. government valued their economic contributions to the region and, to an extent, accepted their way of life. Although the Pueblos lost a good deal of territory to the Americans, they were not banished from their homeland and moved to a reservation. After three centuries of outside invasion, settlement, and cultural destruction, they were still united as a people, and their culture remained alive. ▲

For years, Edward S. Curtis photographed American Indians, such as this Zuni girl in 1903, capturing vivid detail and expression in his portraits.

CHAPTER 8

Facing the Future

By the end of the 19th century, non-Indian settlements increased unabated and the Pueblos found their land holdings significantly reduced. At the same time, outside interest in the Pueblos' ancient and contemporary ways of life was growing. Between 1876 and 1904, displays of Pueblo artifacts and activities—including Indians performing traditional everyday tasks—could be found at many fairs. When the railroads were extended to New Mexico and Arizona in 1880, many people who were curious about the land and the Indians out West came to visit as tourists.

Tourism was a mixed blessing for the Pueblos. It gave them much-needed income but took away their privacy. Tourists were interested in buying traditional Pueblo crafts, and the sale of pottery, jewelry, and paintings became important to the Pueblo economy. The fame of Pueblo pottery grew, and Pueblo artists such as Maximiliana Martinez, Antonita Roybal, Ramona Gonzales, Maria and Julian Martinez, and their son Popovi Da received international recognition for their artwork.

Archaeologists dug up remains of the Pueblos' ancestors to learn about Pueblo life and culture. Now, many Indians prefer to preserve such remains rather than disturb them.

The Pueblos—whose traditional Indian cultures was one of the best-preserved in the United States—were also visited by *archaeologists* and *anthropologists* eager to study Pueblo religion and culture. Although these scholars expressed interest only in documenting, not changing, the Pueblo religion, they were distrusted by the Pueblos, who had learned to be protective of their religion. They especially did not want information published about their sacred rites. Archaeological digs, however, often provided Pueblo men with much-needed jobs, and various discoveries made the Indians even more interested in preserving their history and culture.

Unfortunately, outside visitors brought renewed epidemics of diseases such as tuberculosis, smallpox, and trachoma, which causes blindness. The health care available to the Pueblos was very poor, and these diseases spread quickly.

The question of land ownership remained the Pueblos' biggest problem. There were 12,000 non-Indians living on Pueblo land, much of which had once been farmland. As a result, the Pueblos could no longer produce enough crops to support themselves, and they were forced to depend even more on tourism and wage labor to survive.

Then, in 1910, non-Indians in Congress who were sympathetic to the Pueblos' plight passed the New Mexico Enabling Act to protect the Pueblos' land. In a ruling that created an uproar in New Mexico, the U.S. Supreme Court upheld the act, which declared all land sales since 1848 invalid. Thousands of non-Indians suddenly found themselves living illegally on Indian land. The resulting disputes were not settled until passage of the 1924 Pueblo Lands Act. Under this act, all land owned by non-Indian settlers was returned to the Pueblos unless the settlers could prove they had owned the land for at least 20 years. The Pueblos received money from the government for any lost land and the water on it. They used these funds to purchase other land and to build irrigation projects.

These unprecedented victories resulted in an anti-Indian backlash in the 1920s. Non-Indians in the U.S. government who felt the Pueblos should be forced to live like white Americans got the upper hand. The result was a new wave of intolerance for Pueblo culture, particularly Pueblo religion. The Bureau of Indian Affairs wanted all Indians to take up farming and Christianity in order to blend into American society. Indian children were given Christian religious training in school and were encouraged to abandon traditional Pueblo values. On February 24, 1923, Charles H. Burke, U.S. commissioner of Indian affairs, wrote to the Pueblos and asked them to give up their dances and religious practices within one year. Although he requested that they give up these practices voluntarily, he implied that he might force them to do so if they did not comply.

A Pueblo council wrote back on May 1, 1924. The Pueblos stated that they were being denied religious freedom and that they had no intention of giving up their religion. But the U.S. government kept after them, outlawing "pagan" activities and sending investigators to the pueblos to report any violations. The Pueblos became even more secretive, performing religious ceremonies that were normally held outdoors in underground kivas and barring non-Indians from the pueblos on holy days.

In 1933, a new, more sympathetic commissioner of Indian affairs named John Collier was appointed. He insisted that some of the federal money for social programs under President Franklin D. Roosevelt's *New Deal* be used for Native Americans. Collier was also a supporter of the federal Indian Reorganization Act (IRA) of 1934, which protected Indian lands and in some cases made reservations bigger. It gave monetary credit for

agricultural and industrial projects and dis-
pensed funds for college and technical training. The IRA also encouraged Indians to
change their form of self-government into
one that, like the U.S. government, separated
religious and political life. Collier and other
U.S. officials maintained that changing the
Indians' form of self-government would make
them more self-sufficient. The Pueblos
preferred their old form of government,
which linked political power and religious
authority and had kept them self-sufficient
for centuries.

During World War II, many Pueblos served
in the U.S. armed forces, and those veterans
who returned to Pueblo country often took
advantage of the G.I. Bill, which funded veterans who wished to go to school or to start
businesses. An increasing number of Pueblos began to seek higher education. In the
1950s, a federal relocation program was
created in another attempt to assimilate the
Pueblos into American culture. The program
moved some Pueblos from their homelands
to one of six urban areas: Los Angeles; San
Francisco–Oakland–San Jose; Denver;
Dallas–Fort Worth; Chicago; or Cleveland.
But the Indians often did not get the high-
paying jobs in the city that they had been
promised, and most of those who took part

While the Pueblos have on the surface largely merged into non-Indian society, they maintain close communal and familial ties, keeping traditional Pueblo values alive.

in this program moved back to their homelands after a short time.

During the presidencies of John F. Kennedy and Lyndon B. Johnson, more federal programs were developed for Indians. For the Pueblos, these programs meant funds for new schools and building projects. Tourism continued to grow in importance as a source of money for the Pueblos, and they became famous for their artistry, especially their unique and beautiful pottery.

One of the most significant victories in modern Pueblo history took place in 1970 when President Richard M. Nixon signed a bill deeding 48,000 acres of Carson National Forest in northern New Mexico to the Taos Pueblos. The Taos had been working for 64 years to regain legal control of this territory, which holds great religious and economic value for them.

For the last two decades of the 20th century, Pueblo life has been shaped by the same economic situations as the rest of the United States. The government spends less money on social welfare programs, which has caused some hardship for the Pueblos. As in the rest of America, many jobs have been lost in Pueblo country, and many Indians have migrated to the cities. Pueblo leaders, looking for additional sources of income, have started new businesses, such as bingo parlors, to support their communities. The changes in the Pueblo economy over the last 100 years have changed family life as well. Children no longer tend fields as part of their morning chores, working side by side with their elders. Though their familial ties remain strong, many Pueblos no longer live with their extended families. They gather together on feast days, which are an important way to celebrate family and community connections.

The Pueblos have survived the Spanish conquistadores, European and American settlers, and the loss of much of their land. Through hard times, they have supported their valuable traditions with a determination that has *confounded* both conquerors and missionaries. They have adapted elements of Spanish, Mexican, and American cultures, but have not lost their own culture, identity, or ties to their homeland. Modern Pueblos may drive cars and live in cities, but they maintain close communal ties and traditional Pueblo values. Despite change, the Pueblos still believe that, as the Great Spirit told them so long ago, they are one people and will be so forever. ▲

GLOSSARY

adamant strongly insistent

adobe a building material made of sun-dried earth and straw

anthropologist one who studies human beings and their cultures

archaeologist one who unearths such objects as tools, bones, and pottery of another era to help discover what life used to be like

auxiliary a member of a military force serving a foreign government

confound to confuse or frustrate

conquistadores Spanish forces who conquered most of South and Central America and parts of North America in the 16th century

deploy to put into action, especially for military use

diplomacy peaceful negotiations between groups

dwindle to become smaller over time

extort to obtain through force or the threat of force

kachinas sacred beings in Pueblo mythology who may grant people good fortune and carry their prayers to the gods

kivas large, usually circular, underground chambers in which some Pueblo religious ceremonies are held

lure to attract with a promise of pleasure or gain

mica a semitransparent crystalline rock that separates into thin sheets

New Deal a group of programs enacted during Franklin D. Roosevelt's presidency designed to improve the national economy through federal aid

pueblo the Spanish word for "village," which the Spanish conquistadores used to name all the Indians who lived in the impressive local stone-and-adobe villages

shipapu a sacred spot connecting the upper world, where the Pueblos now live, with the underworld, where they originated and where they will return when they die

viceroy governor of a territory who represents the reigning king or queen

CHRONOLOGY

ca. 1500s   Spanish conquistadores begin exploring the American Southwest in search of gold and silver

1610   Spain claims the Pueblos' territory as a Spanish royal colony

1680   Pueblo revolt, led by Popé, drives the Spanish from Santa Fe

1692   Spanish reclaim Santa Fe; Pueblos divided in their response

1706   Pueblo leaders and the Spanish governor make peace

ca. 1730s   Pueblos join forces with Spanish to battle raids by rival tribes

ca. 1770s   Spanish reach truce with the hostile tribes

1811   Spanish government grants the Pueblos full rights as Spanish citizens and removes special legal protection of Pueblo land

1821   Mexican government gains control of the New Mexico territory but does not interfere with Pueblos

1822   The Santa Fe Trail opens, making American goods more available to the Pueblos

1848   Mexico suffers defeat in the Mexican-American War; cedes New Mexico to the United States

1850   New Mexico is officially declared a U.S. territory; no legal protection is given to Pueblo land

ca. 1880   Railroads extend to New Mexico and Arizona, bringing tourists curious about the Pueblos

1910   The U.S. Congress passes the New Mexico Enabling Act

1924   The U.S. Congress adopts the Pueblo Lands Act

1934   Adoption of the U.S. Indian Reorganization Act, which concerns land protection, self-government, and access to federal funds

ca. 1950s   Federal relocation program fails to integrate Pueblos and other Indians into urban areas nationwide

1970   President Nixon signs bill that returns 48,000 acres of Carson National Forest in New Mexico to the Taos Pueblos

INDEX

N

Nambe pueblo, 11
Navajo Indians, 41, 47, 56, 57,
     62, 63
New Deal, 71
New Mexico, 10, 11, 14, 26, 31,
     42, 45, 49, 51, 52, 53, 54, 56,
     59, 60, 67, 70, 74
New Mexico Enabling Act, 70
Niza, Fray Marcos de, 14, 15

O

Oñate, Don Juan de, 26, 27, 29

P

Pecos River, 24
Popé, 42, 43
Prayer sticks, 42
Pueblo Indians
  agriculture, 7, 41, 46, 60, 61, 63
  architecture, 7, 8, 55
  and Christianity, 14, 16, 19, 21,
       23, 29, 31–32, 41–43
  education, 72, 73
  enslavement, 26, 27, 30, 31, 45
  epidemics, 41, 48, 57, 62, 69
  and famine, 27, 41, 43, 48
  hunting, 7, 55
  and Indian raids, 41, 43, 47, 48, 51
  irrigation methods, 7, 8, 41, 46,
       56, 64, 70
  language, 8, 9, 10, 46
  myths and legends, 7–11
  pottery, 25, 56, 64, 68, 73
  rebellions, 18, 27, 42
  relations with non-Indians, 13–
       49, 53–57, 59–75
  religion, 8, 10, 23, 32, 42, 47,
       53, 69, 70, 71, 72, 74
  textiles, 23, 64
  tourism, 68, 69, 73
  trade with Comanches, 52, 63
  warfare, 47, 48, 49, 62
Pueblo Lands Act, 70

Q

Quivira, 19

R

Railroads, 67
Rebellion of 1680, 42–43, 45, 46
Rio Grande, 8, 11, 23, 26, 61
Rio Grande valley, 9, 10, 21, 24,
     26, 42, 48
Roosevelt, Franklin D., 71
Roybal, Antonita, 68

S

San Ildefonso pueblo, 11
San Juan pueblo, 11, 26, 42
Santa Fe, New Mexico, 42, 43,
     45, 47, 48, 56, 59, 62
Santa Fe Trail, 64
Santo Domingo pueblo, 11, 26
Smallpox, 41, 48, 57, 62, 69
Spain, 14, 16, 53
Spanish, the, 10, 13–53, 60, 62,
     75
Supreme Court, U.S., 70

T

Taos pueblo, 11, 48, 74
Tewa Indians, 42
Tiguex province, 16, 17, 18
Trachoma, 69
Tuberculosis, 69

U

United States, 51, 59, 60, 69, 74
Ute Indians, 47, 56

Y

Yuma Indians, 15

Z

Zuni Indians, 14, 15, 62, 63
Zuni pueblo, 11, 57

ABOUT THE AUTHOR

LIZA N. BURBY is a writer and editor who lives in East Northport, New York.

PICTURE CREDITS

Barker Texas History Center: pp. 12–13; Drawing by Kenneth Chapman, Courtesy the Museum of New Mexico: pp. 16–17 (neg. #48918); Photo by Edward S. Curtis, Courtesy the Museum of New Mexico: pp. 20 (neg. #143735), 66 (neg. #144735); Courtesy Department of Library Services, American Museum of Natural History: p. 24 (neg. #119748); Photo by John K. Hillers, Courtesy the Museum of New Mexico: p. 58 (neg. #31453); Library of Congress: pp. 2, 30, 42, 44, 49; ©Buddy Mays/TRAVEL STOCK: pp. 6, 33–40, 73; Courtesy the Museum of New Mexico: pp. 22 (neg. #74745), 47 (neg. #53602), 52 (neg. #4641), 61 (neg. #37450); Photo by T. Harmon Parkhurst, Courtesy the Museum of New Mexico: p. 28 (neg. #3860); Courtesy Peabody Museum, Harvard University: p. 68 (neg. #N29498); Map by Nicholas Sanson, Courtesy the Museum of New Mexico: p. 18 (neg. #108653); Smithsonian Institution: pp. 8, 9, 54, 55; Photo by Carl N. Werntz, Courtesy the Museum of New Mexico: p. 65 (neg. #147226); Photo by Ben Wittick, Courtesy the Museum of New Mexico: p. 50 (neg. #16004).

P9-DHS-639

15.99
10-5-07
CAN

Emily Post

EMILY'S MAGIC WORDS

Please, Thank You, and More

By Cindy Post Senning, Ed.D., and Peggy Post

Illustrated by Leo Landry

Collins

An Imprint of HarperCollins Publishers

CLINTON-MACOMB PUBLIC LIBRARY

For Casey, Jeep, Dan, and Will
—P.P. and C.P.S.

For Mary and Sophie
—L.L.

Collins is an imprint of HarperCollins Publishers.

Emily's Magic Words: Please, Thank You, and More
Text copyright © 2007 by Cindy Post Senning and Peggy Post
Illustrations copyright © 2007 by Leo Landry
Manufactured in China.

All rights reserved. No part of this book may be used or reproduced in any manner whatsoever without written permission except in the case of brief quotations embodied in critical articles and reviews. For information address HarperCollins Children's Books, a division of HarperCollins Publishers, 1350 Avenue of the Americas, New York, NY 10019.
www.harpercollinschildrens.com

Library of Congress Cataloging-in-Publication Data
Senning, Cindy Post.
   Emily's magic words: pleasae, thank you, and more / by Cindy Post Senning and Peggy Post;
illustrated by Leo Landry. — 1st ed.
     p. cm.
   ISBN-10: 0-06-111680-7 (trade bdg.) — ISBN-13: 978-0-06-111680-3 (trade bdg.)
   ISBN-10: 0-06-111681-5 (lib. bdg.) — ISBN-13: 978-0-06-111681-0 (lib. bdg.)
   1. Etiquette for children and teenagers. I. Senning, Cindy Post. II. Landry, Leo. III. Title.
BJ1857.CSP67 2007   2006019582
395.1'22—dc22   CIP
                                                          AC

Typography by Jeanne L. Hogle
1 2 3 4 5 6 7 8 9 10
❖
First Edition

EMILY'S MAGIC WORDS

Emily can do magic.
Do you know how?

With words!

Magic words!

PLEASE

THANK YOU

GOOD-BYE

HELLO

EXCUSE ME

What makes these
words magic?

Well, they can open doors . . .

Thank you.

These words can make friends . . .

Hello, Jerome!

Hi, Grandma!

How are you, Nutmeg?

even if they disappear from time to time.

These words can turn a frown into a smile . . .

. . . or fix a mistake.

Now that you know Emily's magic words,

you can do magic too!

CLINTON-MACOMB PUBLIC LIBRARY

There are three more magic words.

They are the most magical of all.

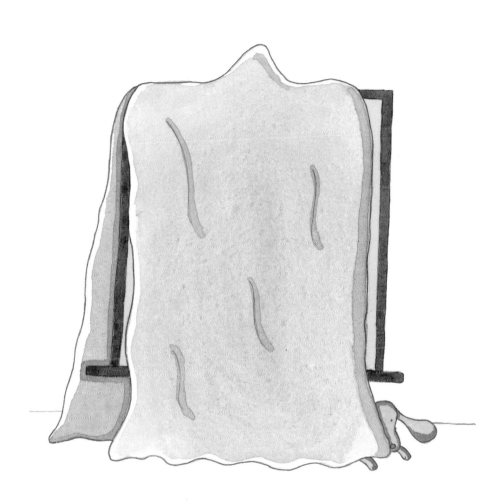

Do you know what they are?

Of course you do!

Note to Parents

ETIQUETTE IS MORE THAN JUST MANNERS AND MAGIC. It is also about three fundamental principles: respect, consideration, and honesty. Even though your toddler is too young to seriously grasp these principles, if you teach basic manners now, you'll be building a climate that reflects respect, consideration, and honesty . . . and magic!

Teaching manners to toddlers can be challenging. They are bundles of energy, curiosity, and unrestrained joy in their widening worlds. They are also beginning to acquire basic social skills—using magic words and table manners, sharing, and taking turns. These are the underpinnings of etiquette and good manners. By helping your toddlers acquire these skills, you are helping them build a firm foundation for all the manners still to come.

There are two basic strategies that should guide you as you teach manners to any child regardless of age:

1. Know what to expect, and then expect it. Take the time to learn what your child is capable of developmentally. Then expect neither too much nor too little!

2. The Golden Rule of Parenting—always behave the way you want your children to behave.

Your children will learn the most from watching you. If you tell them to do one thing and then you do another, they will do what you do, not what you say. Respect them, show them what consideration is, and be honest in the kindest of ways. Then the manners you teach will be meaningful and will last a lifetime.